CRANE CLASSICS

ANDREW MARVELL

SELECTED POEMS

CRANE CLASSICS

Andrew Marvell

Selected Poems

Selected and introduced by
Anthony Eyre

MOUNT ORLEANS
PRESS

Crane Classics Poetry Series
Series editor: Anthony Eyre

This collection first published in 2020 by
Mount Orleans Press
23 High Street, Cricklade SN6 6AP
https://anthonyeyre.com

Volume © 2020 Mount Orleans Press
All rights reserved
"Crane Classics" is a registered trade mark

CIP data for this title are available from the British Library

Typography and book production by Anthony Eyre

ISBN 978-1-912945-19-1

Printed in the UK
by the Short Run Press Ltd
Exeter

Frontispiece:

Andrew Marvell
engraving based on a print by
John Raphael Smith

CONTENTS

ANDREW MARVELL (1621-1678) was born in Wine-
stead, Yorkshire. His father, also Andrew, was a Church
of England clergyman who was moved to Hull Minster as a
Lecturer. It was in Hull that Marvell received his schooling,
at the Grammar School.

Marvell belonged to a younger generation than his fellow
Metaphysical poets John Donne and George Herbert. Like
Herbert he went to Trinity College Cambridge, but he grad-
uated in in 1639 at the age of 18, whereas Herbert had
graduated in 1616 aged 23. Marvell also contrasted with
Herbert in leading what might be seen as a more wordly
life: he travelled widely. For six years from 1642 he trav-
elled the Continent, thus missing a large part of the Civil
War (1642-1651). He certainly went to Rome, but apart
from that it is not known exactly which countries he visited,
though Milton maintained he had fluency in four lan-
guages, including French, Italian and Spanish. Later in life
he again went travelling. In 1656 he took William Dutton,
Cromwell's ward to whom he served as tutor, to visit the
French Protestant Academy at Saumur. After 1659 he went
on behalf of the Hull Trinity House guild to Holland in one
trip and to Sweden, Russia and Denmark in another.

During and after his life Marvell was considered more
important as a political commentator than as a poet. He was
elected MP for Kingston-upon-Hull in 1659 in the Third
Protectorate Parliament, holding the seat for a total of five
Parliaments until his death. At this stage his prose writing,
such as his political satire *The Rehearsal Transpos'd*, was
better known than his poetry, much of which was not pub-
lished until after his death. His lead into a political life was

probably helped by the jobs he held: around about 1650 he became the tutor to the daughter of the Lord General Thomas Fairfax, Commander of the Parliamentary army in the Civil War. Later he undertook the role of tutor to Cromwell's ward, William Dutton. These associations brought about a maturing of his political views, moving the instinctive monarchist to a greater appreciation of the Parliamentarian side. This process can be seen in his 'Horatian Ode' (page 60) where his sympathy for Charles I (*As if his highest plott, To plant the bergamott*) is balanced by his growing admiration of Cromwell – *How good he is, how just, And fit for highest trust.*

It was at Appleton House with the Fairfax family that Marvell's first major poem dates: 'Upon Appleton House'. It anticipates poets such as Dryden and Pope in its style and themes, the house as expression and reflection of the values of the owner, so just as he can say of the building

> And yet what need there here excuse
> Where ev'ry thing does answer use?

so of Fairfax

> For he did, with his utmost skill,
> Ambition weed, but conscience till

the gardening metaphor being typically apt.

Sensuality is a key component of Marvell's poetry, not just famously with the worms in 'To His Coy Mistress', but throughout his love poetry, in the Mower poems and in throw-away lines – *Black eyes, red lips, and curled hair.* Marvell is attractive for his vulnerable humanity, delightfully expressed:

> What but a soul could have the wit
> To build me up for sin so fit?

From

UPON APPLETON HOUSE

To My Lord Fairfax

I

WITHIN this sober frame expect
　　Work of no forrain architect;
That unto caves the quarries drew,
And forrests did to pastures hew;
Who, of his great design in paid,
Did for a model vault his brain;
Whose columns should so high be rais'd,
To arch the brows which on them gaz'd.

II

Why should, of all things, man, unrul'd,
Such unproportion'd dwellings build?
The beasts are by their denns exprest,
And birds contrive an equal nest;
The low-roof'd tortoises do dwell
In cases fit of tortoise-shell:
No creature loves an empty space;
Their bodies measure out their place.

III

But he, superfluously spread,
Demands more room alive than dead;
And in his hollow palace goes,
Where winds, as he, themselves may lose.
What need of all this marble crust,
T'impark the wanton mole of dust,
That thinks by breadth the world t'unite,
Though the first builders fail'd in height?

I V

But all things are composèd here,
Like nature, orderly, and near;
In which we the dimensions find
Of that more sober age and mind,
When larger-sized men did stoop
To enter at a narrow loop;
As practising, in doors so strait,
To strain themselves through Heaven's gate.

V I

Humility alone designs
Those short but admirable lines,
By which, ungirt and unconstrain'd,
Things greater are in less contain'd.
Let others vainly strive t'immure
The circle in the quadrature!
These holy mathematics can
In ev'ry figure equal man.

V I I

Yet thus the laden house does sweat,
And scarce indures the Master great:
But, where he comes, the swelling Hall
Stirs, and the Square grows spherical;
More by his magnitude distrest,
Than he is by its straitness prest:
And too officiously it slights,
That in it self, which him delights.

ANDREW MARVELL

VIII

So Honour better lowness bears,
Than that, unwanted greatness wears;
Height with a certain grace does bend,
But low things clownishly ascend.
And yet what need there here excuse,
Where ev'ry thing does answer use?
Where Neatness nothing can condemn,
Nor Pride invent what to contemn?

IX

A stately frontispiece of poor
Adorns without the open door;
Nor less the rooms within commends
Daily new furniture of friends.
The house was built upon the place,
Only as for a mark of grace,
And for an inn to entertain
Its lord awhile, but not remain.

XI

While with slow Eyes we these survey,
And on each pleasant footstep stay,
We opportunly may relate
The progress of this Houses Fate.
A nunnery first gave it birth
(For virgin buildings oft brought forth),
And all that neighbour-ruine shows
The quarries whence this dwelling rose.

XII

Near to this gloomy cloyster's gates
There dwelt the blooming virgin *Thwaites*;
Fair beyond measure, and an heir
Which might Deformity make fair;
And oft she spent the Summer suns
Discoursing with the suttle nunns;
Whence, in these words, one to her weav'd
(As 'twere by chance) thoughts long conceiv'd:

XIII

'Within this holy leisure we
Live innocently, as you see.
These walls restrain the world without,
But hedge our liberty about;
These bars inclose that wider den
Of those wild creatures callèd men;
The cloyster outward shuts its gates,
And, from us, locks on them the grates.

XIV

Here we, in shining armour white,
Like virgin Amazons do fight,
And our chast lamps we hourly trim,
Lest the Great Bridegroom find them dim.
Our orient breaths perfumèd are
With incense of incessant pray'r;
And holy-water of our tears
Most strangely our complexion clears;

XV

Not tears of grief, but such as those
With which calm Pleasure overflows;
Or Pity, when we look on you
That live without this happy vow.
How should we grieve that must be seen,

ANDREW MARVELL

Each one a spouse, and each a queen;
And you in heaven hence behold
Our brighter robes and crown of gold?

XVI

When we have prayèd all our beads,
Some one the Holy Legend reads;
While all the rest with needles paint
The face and graces of the saint;
But what the linnen can't receive,
They in their lives do interweave.
This work, the saints best represents;
That, serves for altar's ornaments.

XVII

But much it to our work would add,
If here your hand, your face, we had:
By it we would our Lady touch;
Yet thus she you resembles much.
Some of your features, as we sow'd,
Through every shrine should be bestow' d,
And in one beauty we would take
Enough a thousand saints to make.

XVIII

And (for I dare not quench the fire
That me does for your good inspire)
'Twere sacrilege a man t'admit
To holy things, for heaven fit.
I see the angels, in a crown
On you the lillies show'ring down;
And round about you, glory breaks,
That something more than human speaks.
All beauty, when at such a height,
Is so already consecrate.

At the demolishing, this seat,
To *Fairfax* fell, as by escheat;
And what both nuns and Founders will'd,
'Tis likely better thus fulfull'd.
For if the virgin prov'd not theirs,
The cloyster yet remainèd hers;
Though many a nun there made her vow,
'Twas no Religious House till now.

X X X V I

From that blest bed the heroe came
Whom France and Poland yet does fame;
Who, when retirèd here to peace,
His warlike studies could not cease;
But laid these gardens out in sport
In the just figure of a fort;
And with five bastions it did fence,
As aiming one for ev'ry sense.

X X X V I I

When in the east the morning ray
Hangs out the colours of the Day,
The bee through these known alleys hums,
Beating the dian with its drumms.
Then flow'rs their drowsie eylids raise,
Their silken ensigns each displayes,
And dries its pan yet dank with dew,
And fills its flask with odours new.

X X X V I I I

These, as their Governour goes by,
In fragrant volleyes they let fly;
And to salute their Governess

Again as great a charge they press:
None for the virgin Nymph; for she
Seems with the flow'rs a flow'r to be.
And think so still! though not compare
With breath so sweet, or cheek so faire.

XXXIX

Well shot, ye firemen! O how sweet
And round your equal fires do meet;
Whose shrill report no ear can tell,
But ecchoes to the eye and smell.
See how, the flow'rs, as at parade,
Under their colours stand displaid;
Each regiment in order grows,
That of the tulip, pinke, and rose.

XL

But when the vigilant patroul
Of stars walk round about the pole,
Their leaves, which to the stalks are curl'd,
Seem to their staves the ensigns furl'd.
Then in some flow'rs beloved hut,
Each bee, as sentinel, is shut,
And sleeps so too, but if once stir'd,
She runs you through, nor asks the word.

XLI

O thou, that dear and happy Isle,
The garden of the world erewhile,
Thou Paradise of the four seas,
Which heaven planted us to please,
But, to exclude the world, did guard
With watry, if not flaming sword,—
What luckless apple did we tast,
To make us mortal, and thee waste?

XLII

Unhappy! shall we never more
That sweet militia restore,
When gardens only had their towrs,
And all the garrisons were flowrs,
When roses only arms might bear,
And men did rosie garlands wear?
Tulips, in several colours barr'd,
Were then the Switzers of our Guard;

XLIII

The gardiner had the souldier's place,
And his more gentle forts did trace;
The nursery of all things green
Was then the only magazeen;
The Winter quarters were the stoves,
Where he the tender plants removes.
But War all this doth overgrow:
We Ord'nance plant, and powder sow.

XLIV

And yet there walks one on the sod,
Who, had it pleased him and God,
Might once have made our gardens spring,
Fresh as his own, and flourishing.
But he preferr' d to the Cinque Ports,
These five imaginary forts;
And, in those half-dry trenches, spann'd
Pow'r which the ocean might command.

XLV

For he did, with his utmost skill,
Ambition weed, but conscience till:
Conscience, that heaven-nursèd plant,
Which most our earthly gardens want.
A prickling leaf it bears, and such

ANDREW MARVELL

As that which shrinks at ev'ry touch,
But flowers eternal, and divine,
That in the crowns of saints do shine.

XLVI

The sight does from these bastions ply,
Th'invisible artilery,
And at proud Cawood Castle seems
To point the battery of its beams;
As if it quarrell'd in the seat,
Th'ambition of its prelate great,
But o'er the meads below it plays,
Or innocently seems to gaze.

XLVII

And now the abbyss I pass
Of the unfathomable grass,
Where men like grasshoppers appear,
But grasshoppers are gyants there:
They, in their squeking laugh, contemn
Us as we walk more low then them:
And, from the Precipices tall
Of the green spir's, to us do call.

LI

But bloody Thestylis, that waites
To bring the mowing camp their cates,
Greedy as kites, has trust it up,
And forthwith means on it to sup;
When on another quick she lights,
And cryes, 'He call'd us Israelites;
But now, to make his saying true,
Rails rain for quails, for manna dew.'

Unhappy birds! what does it boot
To build below the grasse's root;
When lowness is unsafe as hight,
And chance o'retakes what 'scapeth spight?
And now your orphan parents' call
Sounds your untimely funeral;
Death-trumpets creak in such a note,
And 'tis the sourdine in their throat.

L I I I

Or sooner hatch, or higher build;
The mower now commands the field,
In whose new traverse seemeth wrought
A camp of battail newly fought;
Where, as the meads with hay, the plain
Lyes quilted o'er with bodies slain;
The women that with forks it fling,
Do represent the pillaging.

L I V

And now the careless victors play,
Dancing the triumphs of the hay;
Where every mower's wholesome heat,
Smells like an *Alexander's* sweat,
Their females, fragrant as the mead
Which they in fairy circles tread:
When at their dances' end they kiss,
Their new-made hay not sweeter is.

L V

When, after this, 'tis pil'd in cocks,
Like a calm sea it shews the rocks,
We wondring in the river near
How boats among them safely steer:
Or, like the desert Memphis' sand,

ANDREW MARVELL

Short pyramids of hay do stand;
And such the Roman camps do rise
In hills for soldiers' obsequies.

LXV

The nightingale does here make choice
To sing the tryals of her voice;
Low shrubs she sits in, and adorns
With musick high the squatted thorns;
But highest oakes stoop down to hear,
And listning elders prick the ear;
The thorn, lest it should hurt her, draws
Within the skin its shrunken claws.

LXVI

But I have for my musick found
A sadder, yet more pleasing sound;
The stock-doves, whose fair necks are grac'd
With nuptial rings, their ensigns chast;
Yet always, for some cause unknown,
Sad pair, unto the elms they moan:
O why should such a couple mourn,
That in so equal flames do burn!

LXVII

Then as I careless on the bed
Of gelid strawberryes do tread,
And through the hazies thick espy
The hatching throstle's shining eye;
The heron, from the ashe's top,
The eldest of its young lets drop,
As if it stork-like did pretend
That tribute to its lord to send.

LXVIII

But most the hewel's wonders are,
Who here has the holt-felster's care;
He walks still upright from the root,
Meas'ring the timber with his foot;
And all the way, to keep it clean,
Doth from the bark the wood-moths glean;
He, with his beak, examines well
Which fit to stand, and which to fell;

LXIX

The good he numbers up, and hacks
As if he mark'd them with the ax;
But where he, tinkling with his beak,
Does find the hollow oak to speak,
That for his building he designs,
And through the tainted side he mines.
Who could have thought the tallest oak
Should fall by such a feeble strok?

LXX

Nor would it, had the tree not fed
A traitor-worm, within it bred;
(As first our flesh, corrupt within,
Tempts impotent and bashful Sin;)
And yet that worm triumphs not long,
But serves to feed the hewel's young,
While the oake seems to fall content,
Viewing the treason's punishment.

LXXI

Thus, I, easie philosopher,
Among the birds and trees confer;
And little now to make me wants
Or of the fowles, or of the plants:

ANDREW MARVELL

Give me but wings as they, and I
Streight floting on the air shall fly;
Or turn me but, and you shall see
I was but an inverted tree.

LXXII

Already I begin to call
In their most learned original,
And, where I language want, my signs
The bird upon the bough divines;
And more attentive there doth sit
Than if she were with lime-twigs knit.
No leaf does tremble in the wind,
Which I returning cannot find.

LXXIII

Out of these scatter'd Sibyls' leaves,
Strange prophecies my phancy weaves,
And in one history consumes,
Like Mexique paintings, all the plumes;
What Rome, Greece, Palestine, ere said,
I in this light Mosaick read.
Thrice happy he, who, not mistook,
Hath read in Nature's mystick book!

LXXIV

And see, how Chance's better wit
Could with a mask my studies hit;
The oak-leaves me embroyder all,
Between which caterpillars crawl;
And ivy, with familiar trails,
Me licks and clasps, and curles and hales.
Under this antick cope I move,
Like some great prelate of the grove;

LXXV

Then, languished with ease, I toss
On pallets swoln of velvet moss;
While the wind, cooling through the boughs,
Flatters with air my panting brows.
Thanks for my rest, ye mossy banks,
And unto you, cool zephyrs, thanks,
Who, as my hair, my thoughts too shed,
And winnow from the chaff my head!

LXXVI

How safe, methinks, and strong, behind
These trees, have I incamped my mind;
Where Beauty, aiming at the heart,
Bends in some tree its useless dart,
And where the world no certain shot
Can make, or me it toucheth not,
But I on it securely play,
And gaul its horsemen all the day.

LXXVII

Bind me, ye woodbines, in your 'twines,
Curle me about, ye gadding vines,
And oh so close your circles lace,
That I may never leave this place:
But, lest your fetters prove too weak,
Ere I your silken bondage break,
Do you, O brambles, chain me too,
And, courteous briars, nail me through!

LXXVIII

Here in the morning tye my chain,
Where the two woods have made a lane;
While, like a guard on either side,
The trees before their lord divide;

ANDREW MARVELL

This, like a long and equal thread,
Betwixt two labyrinths does lead.
But, where the floods did lately drown,
There, at the ev'ning, stake me down;

L X X I X
For now the waves are fall'n and dry'd,
And now the meadows fresher dy'd,
Whose grass, with moister colour dasht,
Seems as green silks but newly washt.
No serpent new, nor crocodile,
Remains behind our little Nile;
Unless it self you will mistake,
Among these meads the only snake.

L X X X
See in what wanton harmless folds,
It ev'rywhere the meadow holds,
And its yet muddy back doth lick,
'Till as a chrystal mirrour slick,
Where all things gaze themselves, and doubt
If they be in it, or without;
And for his shade which therein shines,
Narcissus-like, the sun too pines.

L X X X I
Oh what a pleasure 'tis to hedge
My temples here with heavy sedge;
Abandoning my lazy side,
Stretcht as a bank unto the tide;
Or to suspend my sliding foot
On th' osier's undermined root,
And in its branches tough to hang,
While at my lines the fishes twang!

LXXXII

But now away my hooks, my quills,
And angles, idle utensils!
The young *Maria* walks to-night:
Hide, trifling youth, thy pleasures slight:
'Twere shame that such judicious eyes
Should with such toyes a man surprise;
She that already is the law
Of all her sex, her age's aw.

LXXXIII

See how loose Nature, in respect
To her, it self doth recollect;
And every thing so whisht and fine,
Starts, forthwith, into its bonne mine.
The sun himself of her aware,
Seems to descend with greater care;
And, lest she see him go to bed,
In blushing clouds conceales his head.

LXXXIV

So when the shadows laid asleep,
From underneath these banks do creep,
And on the river, as it flows,
With eben shuts begin to close,
The modest halcyon comes in sight,
Flying betwixt the day and night;
And such a horror calm and dumb,
Admiring Nature does benum;

LXXXV

The viscous air, wheres're she fly,
Follows and sucks her azure dy;
The gellying stream compacts below,
If it might fix her shadows so;

The stupid fishes hang, as plain
As flies in chrystal overt'ane;
And men the silent scene assist,
Charm' d with the saphir-winged mist.

XCIV

Meantime, ye fields, springs, bushes, flow'rs,
Where yet she leads her studious hours;
Employ the means you have by her,
And in your kind your selves preferr;
That, as all virgins she preceds,
So you all woods, streams, gardens, meads.

XCV

For you Thessalian Tempe's seat
Shall now be scorn'd as obsolete;
Aranjeuz, as less, disdai'd;
The Bel-Retiro, as constrain'd,
But name not the Idalian grove,
For 'twas the seat of wanton love;
Nor e'en the dead's Elysian Fields;
Yet not to them your beauty yields.

XCVI

'Tis not what once it was, the world,
But a rude heap together hurl'd,
All negligently overthrown,
Gulfes, deserts, precipices, stone:
Your lesser world contains the same,
But in more decent order tame;
You, Heaven's center, Nature's lap;
And Paradise's only map.

And now the salmon-fishers moist,
Their leathern boats begin to hoist;
And, like Antipodes in shoes,
Have shod their heads in their canoos.
How tortoise-like, but not so low,
These rational amphibii go!
Let's in; for the dark hemisphere
Does now like one of them appear.

THE GARDEN

Hᴏᴡ ᴠᴀɪɴʟʏ men themselves amaze,
To win the palm, the oak, or bayes;
And their uncessant labours see
Crown'd from some single herb or tree,
Whose short and narrow-vergèd shade
Does prudently their toyles upbraid;
While all the flow'rs and trees do close,
To weave the garlands of repose.

Fair Quiet, have I found thee here,
And Innocence, thy sister dear!
Mistaken long, I sought you then
In busie companies of men.
Your sacred plants, if here below,
Only among the plants will grow;
Society is all but rude
To this delicious solitude.

No white nor red was ever seen
So am'rous as this lovely green.
Fond lovers, cruel as their flame,
Cut in these trees their mistress' name:
Little, alas! they know or heed,
How far these beauties her's exceed!
Fair trees, wheres'eer your barkes I wound,
No name shall but your own be found.

When we have run our passions' heat,
Love hither makes his best retreat.
The gods, who mortal beauty chase,
Still in a tree did end their race;

Apollo hunted Daphne so,
Only that she might laurel grow;
And Pan did after Syrinx speed,
Not as a nymph, but for a reed.

What wond'rous life is this I lead!
Ripe apples drop about my head;
The luscious clusters of the vine
Upon my mouth do crush their wine;
The nectaren and curious peach,
Into my hands themselves do reach;
Stumbling on melons, as I pass,
Insnar'd with flow'rs, I fall on grass.

Meanwhile the mind, from pleasure less,
Withdrawn into its happiness;
The mind, that ocean where each kind
Does straight its own resemblance find;
Yet it creates—transcending these—
Far other worlds and other seas;
Annihilating all that's made
To a green thought in a green shade.

Here at the fountain's sliding foot,
Or at some fruit-tree's mossy root,
Casting the bodie's vest aside,
My soul into the boughs does glide:
There, like a bird it sits, and sings,
Then whets and claps its silver wings;
And, till prepar'd for longer flight,
Waves in its plumes the various light.

Such was that happy garden-state,
While man there walk'd without a mate:
After a place so pure and sweet,
What other help could yet be meet!

ANDREW MARVELL

But 'twas beyond a mortal's share
To wander solitary there:
Two paradises 'twere in one,
To live in paradise alone.

How well the skilful gardner drew
Of flow'rs and herbs this dial new;
Where, from above, the milder sun
Does through a fragrant zodiack run,
And, as it works, th'industrious bee
Computes its time as well as we!
How could such sweet and wholsome hours
Be reckon'd but with herbs and flow'rs!

THE MOWER, AGAINST GARDENS

LUXURIOUS MAN, to bring his vice in use,
Did after him the world seduce,
And from the fields the flow'rs and plants allure,
    Where Nature was most plain and pure.
He first enclos'd within the gardens square
    A dead and standing pool of air;
And a more luscious earth for them did knead,
    Which stupefi'd them while it fed.
The pink grew then as double as his mind;
    The nutriment did change the kind.
With strange perfumes he did the roses taint;
    And flow'rs themselves were taught to paint.
The tulip, white, did for complexion seek,
    And learn'd to interline its cheek;
Its onion-root they then so high did hold,
    That one was for a meadow sold:
Another world was search'd through oceans new,
    To find the marvel of Peru;

And yet these rarities might be allow'd
　　To man, that sov'raign thing and proud;
Had he not dealt between the bark and tree,
　　Forbidden mixtures there to see.
No plant now knew the stock from which it came;
　　He grafts upon the wild the tame:
That the uncertain and adult'rate fruit
　　Might put the palate in dispute.
His green seraglio has its eunuchs too,
　　Lest any tyrant him outdoe;
And in the cherry he does Nature vex,
　　To procreate without a sex.
'Tis all enforc'd, the fountain and the grot;
　　While the sweet fields do lye forgot,
Where willing Nature does to all dispence
　　A wild and fragrant innocence,
And fauns and fairyes do the meadows till
　　More by their presence than their skill.
Their statues, polish'd by some ancient hand,
　　May to adorn the gardens stand;
But, howso'ere the figures do excel,
　　The Gods themselves with us do dwell.

　　　　　　　　　　　　　　　ANDREW MARVELL

DAMON THE MOWER

H ARK HOW the mower Damon sung,
With love of Juliana stung!
While every thing did seem to paint
The scene more fit for his complaint:
Like her fair eyes, the day was fair,
But scorching like his am'rous care;
Sharp, like his sythe, his sorrow was,
And whithered, like his hopes, the grass.

Oh what unusual heats are here,
Which thus our sun-burn'd meadows fear!
The grasshopper its pipe gives ore,
And hamstring'd frogs can dance no more;
But in the brook the green frog wades,
And grasshoppers seek out the shades;
Only the snake, that kept within,
Now glitters in its second skin.

I am the mower Damon, known
Through all the meadows I have own.
On me the Morn her dew distills
Before her darling daffodils,
And, if at noon my toil me heat,
The Sun himself licks off my sweat;
While, going home, the ev'ning sweet
In cowslip-water bathes my feet.

What, though the piping shepherd stock
The plains with an unnum'red flock,
This sithe of mine discovers wide
More ground than all his sheep do hide.
With this the golden fleece I shear
Of all these closes ev'ry year,
And though in wooll more poor than they,
Yet I am richer far in hay.

Nor am I so deform'd to sight,
If in my sithe I lookèd right;
In which I see my picture done,
As in a crescent moon the sun.
The deathless fairyes take me oft
To lead them in their danses soft;
And when I tune myself to sing,
About me they contract their ring.

How happy might I still have mow'd,
Had not Love here his thistle sow'd!
But now I all the day complain,
Joining my labour to my pain;
And with my scythe cut down the grass,
Yet still my grief is where it was;
But, when the iron blunter grows,
Sighing I whet my sythe and woes.

While thus he drew his elbow round,
Depopulating all the ground,
And, with his whistling sythe, does cut,
Each stroke between the earth and root,
The edged stele by careless chance,
Did into his own ankle glance;
And there among the grass fell down,
By his own sythe the mower mown.

ANDREW MARVELL

Alas! said he, these hurts are slight
To those that dye by Love's despight.
With shepherd's-purse, and clown's all-heal,
The blood I stanch and wound I seal.
Only for him no cure is found,
Whom Juliana's eyes do wound:
'Tis Death alone that this must do;
For, Death, thou art a Mower too.

THE MOWER TO THE GLO-WORMS

Ye living lamps, by whose dear light
The nightingale does sit so late,
And studying all the summer-night,
Her matchless songs does meditate;

Ye Country Comets, that portend
No war, nor Princes funeral,
Shining unto no higher end
Then to presage the grasses fall;

Ye Glo-worms, whose officious flame
To wandring Mowers shows the way,
That in the night have lost their aim,
And after foolish fires do stray;

Your courteous lights in vain you wast,
Since Juliana here is come,
For She my Mind hath so displac'd
That I shall never find my home.

AMETAS AND THESTYLIS
MAKING HAY-ROPES

Ametas
Think'st Thou that this Love can stand,
Whilst Thou still dost say me nay?
Love unpaid does soon disband:
Love binds Love as Hay binds Hay.

Thestylis
Think'st Thou that this Rope would twine
If we both should turn one way?
Where both parties so combine,
Neither Love will twist nor Hay.

Ametas
Thus you vain Excuses find,
Which your selve and us delay:
And Love tyes a Womans Mind
Looser than with Ropes of Hay.

Thestylis
What you cannot constant hope
Must be taken as you may.

Ametas
Then let's both lay by our Rope,
And go kiss within the Hay.

CLORINDA AND DAMON

Clorinda	DAMON, come drive thy flocks this way.
Damon	No: 'tis too late they went astray.
Clorinda	I have a grassy scutcheon spied,
	Where Flora blazons all her pride;
	The grass I aim to feast thy sheep,

ANDREW MARVELL

	The flowers I for thy temples keep.
Damon	Grass withers, and the flowers too fade.
Clorinda	Seize the short joys then, ere they vade.
	Seest thou that unfrequented cave?
Damon	That den?
Clorinda	Love's shrine.
Damon	But virtue's grave.
Clorinda	In whose cool bosom we may lie,
	Safe from the sun.
Damon	Not Heaven's eye.
Clorinda	Near this, a fountain's liquid bell
	Tinkles within the concave shell.
Damon	Might a soul bathe there and be clean,
	Or slake its drought?
Clorinda	What is't you mean?
Damon	These once had been enticing things,
	Clorinda, pastures, caves, and springs.
Clorinda	And what late change ?
Damon	The other day
	Pan met me.
Clorinda	What did great Pan say ?
Damon	Words that transcend poor shepherd's skill;
	But he e'er since my songs does fill,
	And his name swells my slender oat.
Clorinda	Sweet must Pan sound in Damon's note.
Damon	Clorinda's voice might make it sweet.
Clorinda	Who would not in Pan's praises meet?
Chorus	Of Pan the flowery pastures sing,
	Caves echo, and the fountains ring.
	Sing then while he doth us inspire;
	For all the world is our Pan's quire.

BERMUDAS

WHERE THE remote Bermudas ride,
  In th'ocean's bosome unespy'd,
From a small boat, that row'd along,
The list'ning winds receiv'd this song:
  'What should we do but sing His praise,
That led us through the wat'ry maze,
Unto an isle so long unknown,
And yet far kinder than our own?
Where he the huge sea-monsters wracks,
That lift the deep upon their backs;
He lands us on a grassy stage,
Safe from the storms, and prelat's rage.
He gave us this eternal Spring,
Which here enamells every thing;
And sends the fowls to us in care,
On daily visits through the air;
He hangs in shades the orange bright,
Like golden lamps in a green night;
And does in the pomegranates close,
Jewels more rich than Ormus shows;
He makes the figs our mouths to meet,
And throws the melons at our feet;
But apples, plants of such a price,
No tree could ever bear them twice;
With cedars, chosen by His hand,
From Lebanon, He stores the land;
And makes the hollow seas, that roar,
Proclaim the ambergris on shoar.
He cast (of which we rather boast)
The Gospel's pearl upon our coast,

And in these rocks for us did frame
A temple, where to sound His name.
Oh! let our voice His praise exalt,
'Till it arrive at Heaven's vault;
Which, thence (perhaps) rebounding, may
Eccho beyond the Mexique Bay!'
   Thus sung they, in the English boat,
An holy and a chearful note,
And all the way, to guide their chime,
With falling oars they kept the time.

THE CORONET

WHEN FOR the thorns with which I long, too long,
   With many a piercing wound,
My Saviour's head have crown'd,
I seek with garlands to redress that wrong:
Through every garden, every mead,
I gather flow'rs (my fruits are only flow'rs),
Dismantling all the fragrant towers
That once adorn'd my shepherdesse's head:
And now, when I have summ'd up all my store,
Thinking (so I myself deceive)
So rich a chaplet thence to weave
As never yet the King of Glory wore:
Alas! I find the Serpent old,
That, twining in his speckled breast,
About the flowers disguis'd, does fold
With wreaths of fame and interest.
   Ah! foolish man, that would'st debase with them,
And mortal glory, Heaven's diadem!
But thou who only could'st the Serpent tame,

Either his slipp'ry knots at once untie,
And disintangle all his winding snare;
Or shatter too with him my curious frame,
And let these wither—so that he may die—
Though set with skill, and chosen out with care:
That they, while Thou on both their spoils dost tread,
May crown Thy feet, that could not crown Thy head.

A DIALOGUE BETWEEN THE SOUL
AND BODY

Soul

O WHO SHALL from this dungeon raise
A soul inslav'd so many wayes?
With bolts of bones, that fetter'd stands
In feet, and manacled in hands;
Here blinded with an eye, and there
Deaf with the drumming of an ear;
A soul hung up, as 'twere, in chains
Of nerves, and arteries, and veins;
Tortur'd besides each other part,
In a vain head, and double heart?

Body

O, who shall me deliver whole,
From bonds of this tyrannic soul?
Which, stretcht upright, impales me so
That mine own precipice I go;
And warms and moves this needless frame
(A fever could but do the same),
And, wanting where it spight to try,
Has made me live to let me dye
A body that could never rest
Since this ill spirit it possest.

ANDREW MARVELL

Soul

What magick could me thus confine
Within another's grief to pine?
Where, whatsoever it complain,
I feel, that cannot feel, the pain;
And all my care itself employes,
That to preserve which me destroys:
Constrain'd not only to indure
Diseases, but, what's worse, the cure;
And, ready oft the port to gain,
Am shipwrackt into health again.

Body

But Physick yet could never reach
The maladies thou me dost teach;
Whom first the cramp of Hope does tear,
And then the palsie shakes of Fear;
The pestilence of Love does heat,
Or Hatred's hidden ulcer eat;
Joy's cheerful madness does perplex,
Or Sorrow's other madness vex;
Which knowledge forces me to know,
And memory will not forego;
What but a soul could have the wit
To build me up for sin so fit?
So architects do square and hew
Green trees that in the forest grew.

A DIALOGUE BETWEEN THE RESOLVED
SOUL AND CREATED PLEASURE

COURAGE, MY soul, now learn to wield
  The weight of thine immortal shield;
Close on thy head thy helmet bright,
Balance thy sword against the fight;
See where an army, strong as fair,
With silken banners spread the air!
Now, if thou bee'st that thing divine,
In this day's combat let it shine;
And show that Nature wants an art
To conquer one resolved heart.

Pleasure
Welcome the creation's guest,
Lord of Earth, and Heaven's heir!
Lay aside that warlike crest,
And of Nature's banquet share;
Where the souls of fruits and flow'rs
Stand prepar'd to heighten yours.

Soul
I sup above, and cannot stay,
To bait so long upon the way.

Pleasure
On these downy pillows lye,
Whose soft plumes will thither fly!
On these roses, strow' d so plain
Lest one leaf thy side should strain.

Soul

My gentler rest is on a thought—
Conscious of doing what I ought.

Pleasure

If thou bee'st with perfumes pleas'd,
Such as oft the gods appeas'd,
Thou in fragrant clouds shalt show,
Like another god below.

Soul

A soul that knows not to presume,
Is Heaven's and its own, perfume

Pleasure

Every thing does seem to vie
Which should first attract thine eye:
But since none deserves that grace,
In this crystal view thy face.

Soul

When the Creator's skill is priz'd,
The rest is all but earth disguis'd.

Pleasure

Hark now musick then prepares
For thy stay these charming aires,
Which the posting winds recall,
And suspend the river's fall.

Soul

Had I but any time to lose,
On this I would it all dispose.
Cease tempter! None can chain a mind,
Whom this sweet chordage cannot bind.

Chorus

Earth cannot show so brave a sight,
As when a single soul does fence
The batteries of alluring Sense,
And Heaven views it with delight.
Then persevere; for still new charges sound,
And if thou overcom'st thou shalt be crown'd.

Pleasure

All that's costly, fair, and sweet,
Which scatteringly doth shine,
Shall within one beauty meet,
And she be only thine.

Soul

If things of sight such heavens be,
What heavens are those we cannot see?

Pleasure

Whereso're thy foot shall go
The minted gold shall lie,
Till thou purchase all below,
And want new worlds to buy.

Soul

Wer't not for price who'd value gold?
And that's worth naught that can be sold.

Pleasure

Wilt thou all the glory have
That War or Peace commend?
Half the world shall be thy slave,
The other half thy friend.

ANDREW MARVELL

Soul

What friends, if to myself untrue?
What slaves, unless I captive you?

Pleasure

Thou shalt know each hidden cause,
And see the future time;
Try what depth the centre draws,
And then to heaven climb.

Soul

None thither mounts by the degree
Of knowledge, but humility.

Chorus

Triúmph, triúmph, victorious soul!
The world has not one pleasure more:
The rest does lie beyond the pole,
And is thine everlasting store.

THE GALLERY

CHLORA, COME view my soul, and tell
Whether I have contriv'd it well:
How all its several lodgings lye,
Compos'd into one gallery;
And the great arras-hangings, made
Of various faces, by are laid,
That, for all furniture, you'l find
Only your picture in my mind.
Here thou art painted in the dress
Of an inhumane murtheress;
Examining upon our hearts

(Thy fertile shop of cruel arts)
Engines more keen than ever yet
Adornèd tyrant's cabinet;
Of which the most tormenting are,
Black eyes, red lips, and curled hair.

But, on the other side, th'art drawn,
Like to Aurora in the dawn;
When in the East she slumb'ring lyes,
And stretches out her milky thighs;
While all the morning quire does sing,
And manna falls and roses spring;
And, at thy feet, the wooing doves
Sit perfecting their harmless loves.

Like an enchantress here thou show'st,
Vexing thy restless lover's ghost;
And, by a light obscure, dost rave
Over his entrails, in the cave;
Divining thence, with horrid care,
How long thou shalt continue fair;
And (when inform'd) them throw'st away
To be the greedy vultur's prey.

But, against that, thou sit'st afloat,
Like Venus in her pearly boat;
The halcyons, calming all that's nigh,
Betwixt the air and water fly;
Or, if some rowling wave appears,
A mass of ambergris it bears,
Nor blows more wind, than what may well
Convoy the perfume to the smell.

ANDREW MARVELL

These pictures, and a thousand more,
Of thee, my gallery do store,
In all the forms thou can'st invent,
Either to please me, or torment;
For thou alone, to people me,
Art grown a num'rous colony,
And a collection choicer far
Then or Whitehall's or Mantua's were.

But, of these pictures, and the rest,
That at the entrance likes me best;
Where the same posture, and the look
Remains, with which I first was took;
A tender shepherdess, whose hair
Hangs loosely playing in the air,
Transplanting flow'rs from the green hill
To crown her head, and bosome fill.

THE DEFINITION OF LOVE

I

MY LOVE is of a birth as rare
As 'tis, for object, strange and high;
It was begotten by Despair
Upon Impossibility.

II

Magnanimous Despair alone
Could show me so divine a thing;
Where feeble Hope could ne'r have flown,
But vainly flapt its tinsel wing.

III

And yet I quickly might arrive
Where my extended soul is fixt;
But Fate does iron wedges drive,
And alwaies crowds itself betwixt.

IV

For Fate with jealous eye doth see
Two perfect loves, nor lets them close;
Their union would her ruine be,
And her tyrannick power depose.

V

And therefore her decrees of steel
Us as the distant poles have plac'd
(Though Love's whole world on us doth wheel),
Not by themselves to be embrac'd.

VI

Unless the giddy heaven fall,
And Earth some new convulsion tear,
And, us to join, the world should all
Be cramp'd into a planisphere.

VII

As lines, so loves oblique, may well
Themselves in every angle greet:
But ours, so truly paralel,
Though infinite, can never meet.

VII

Therefore the love which us doth bind,
But Fate so enviously debarrs,
Is the conjunction of the mind,
And opposition of the stars.

TO HIS COY MISTRESS

HAD WE but world enough, and time,
This coyness, lady, were no crime.
We would sit down, and think which way
To walk, and pass out long love's day.
Thou by the Indian Ganges' side
Should'st rubies find: I by the tide
Of Humber would complain. I would
Love you ten years before the Flood,
And you should, if you please, refuse
Till the conversion of the Jews;
My vegetable love should grow
Vaster than empires and more slow;
An hundred years should go to praise
Thine eyes, and on thy forehead gaze;
Two hundred to adore each breast,
But thirty thousand to the rest;
An age at least to every part,
And the last age should show your heart.
For, lady, you deserve this state,
Nor wou[d I love at lower rate.

But at my back I alwaies hear
Time's winged charriot hurrying near;
And yonder all before us lye
Desarts of vast Eternity.
Thy beauty shall no more be found,
Nor, in thy marble vault, shall sound
My ecchoing song; then, worms shall try
That long preserv'd virginity;
And your quaint honour turn to dust,

And into ashes all my lust:
The grave's a fine and private place,
But none, I think, do there embrace.

Now therefore, while the youthful hew
Sits on thy skin like morning dew,
And while thy willing soul transpires
At every pore with instant fires,
Now let us sport us while we may,
And now, like am'rous birds of prey,
Rather at once our time devour,
Than languish in his slow-chapt pow'r.
Let us roll all our strength, and all
Our sweetness up into one ball;
And tear our pleasures with rough strife,
Through the iron gates of life;
Thus, though we cannot make our sun
Stand still, yet we will make him run.

ANDREW MARVELL

A LAS! HOW pleasant are their days,
  With whom the infant love yet plays!
Sorted by pairs, they still are seen
By fountains cool and shadows green ;
But soon these flames do lose their light,
Like meteors of a summer's night;
Nor can they to that region climb,
To make impression upon Time.

'Twas in a shipwreck, when the seas
Ruled, and the winds did what they please,
That my poor lover floating lay,
And, ere brought forth, was cast away;
Till at the last the master wave
Upon the rock his mother drave,
And there she split against the stone,
In a Cæsarian section.

The sea him lent these bitter tears,
Which at his eyes he always bears,
And from the winds the sighs he bore,
Which through his surging breast do roar;
No day he saw but that which breaks
Through frighted clouds in forkèd streaks,
While round the rattling thunder hurled,
As at the funeral of the world.

While Nature to his birth presents
This masque of quarrelling elements,
A numerous fleet of cormorants black,
That sailed insulting o'er the wrack,
Received into their cruel care,
The unfortunate and abject heir;
Guardians most fit to entertain
The orphan of the hurricane.

They fed him up with hopes and air,
Which soon digested to despair,
And as one cormorant fed him, still
Another on his heart did bill;
Thus, while they famish him and feast,
He both consumèd, and increased,
And languishèd with doubtful breath,
The amphibium of life and death.

And now, when angry Heaven would
Behold a spectacle of blood,
Fortune and he are called to play
At sharp before it all the day,
And tyrant Love his breast does ply
With all his winged artillery,
Whilst he, betwixt the flames and waves,
Like Ajax, the mad tempest braves.

See how he nak'd and fierce does stand,
Cuffing the thunder with one hand,
While with the other he does lock,
And grapple, with the stubborn rock;
From which he with each wave rebounds,
Torn into flames, and ragg'd with wounds ;
And all he says, a lover drest
In his own blood does relish best.

This is the only banneret
That ever Love created yet ;
Who, though by the malignant stars,
Forcèd to live in storms and wars,
Yet dying, leaves a perfume here,
And music within every ear ;
And he in story only rules,
In a field sable, a lover gules.

ANDREW MARVELL

THE PICTURE OF LITTLE T.C. IN A
PROSPECT OF FLOWERS

I

SEE WITH what simplicity
This nimph begins her golden daies!
In the green grass she loves to lie,
And there with her fair aspect tames
The wilder flow'rs, and gives them names;
But only with the roses playes,
                                And them does tell
What colours best become them, and what smell.

II

Who can foretel for what high cause,
This darling of the Gods was born?
Yet this is she whose chaster laws
The wanton Love shall one day fear,
And, under her command severe,
See his bow broke, and ensigns torn.
                                Happy who can
Appease this virtuous enemy of man!

III

O, then let me in time compound
And parly with those conquering eyes;
Ere they have try'd their force to wound:
Ere with their glancing wheels they drive
In triumph over hearts that strive,
And them that yield but more despise:
                                Let me be laid,
Where I may see the glories from some shade.

IV

Mean time, whilst every verdant thing
It self does at thy beauty charm,
Reform the arrours of the Spring;
Make that the tulips may have share
Of sweetness, seeing they are fair;
And roses of their thorns disarm;
                But most procure
That violets may a longer age endure.

V

But O, young beauty of the woods,
Whom Nature courts with fruits and flow'rs,
Gather the flow'rs, but spare the buds;
Lest Flora, angry at thy crime
To kill her infants in their prime,
Should quickly make th' example yours:
                And ere we see—
Nip in the blossome—all our hopes and thee.

ANDREW MARVELL

THE FAIR SINGER

To make a final conquest of all me,
Love did compose so sweet an enemy,
In whom both beauties to my death agree,
Joyning themselves in fatal harmony;
That, while she with her eyes my heart does bind,
She with her voice might captivate my mind.

I could have fled from one but singly fair;
My disintangled soul itself might save,
Breaking the curled trammels of her hair;
But how should I avoid to be her slave,
Whose subtile art invisibly can wreath
My fetters of the very air I breathe?

It had been easy fighting in some plain,
Where victory might hang in equal choice;
But all resistance against her is vain,
Who has th'advantage both of eyes and voice;
And all my forces needs must be undone,
She having gainèd both the wind and sun.

MOURNING

I

You, that decipher out the fate
Of humane offsprings from the skies,
What mean these infants which, of late,
Spring from the stars of Chlora's eyes?

II

Her eyes confus'd, and doubled ore
With tears suspended ere they flow,
Seem bending upwards, to restore
To heaven, whence it came, their woe;

III

When, molding of the watry sphears,
Slow drops unty themselves away;
As if she with those precious tears
Would strow the ground where Strephon lay.

IV

Yet some affirm, pretending art,
Her eyes have so her bosome drown'd,
Only to soften, near her heart,
A place to fix another wound.

V

And, while vain pomp does her restrain
Within her solitary bowr,
She courts her self in am'rous rain,
Herself both Danae and the showr.

VI

Nay others, bolder, hence esteem
Joy now so much her master grown,
That whatsoever does but seem
Like grief, is from her windows thrown.

VII

Nor that she payes, while she survives,
To her dead love this tribute due;
But casts abroad donatives,
At the installing of a new.

VIII

How wide they dream! the Indian slaves,
Who sink for pearl through seas profound,
Would find her tears yet deeper waves,
And not of one the bottom sound.

IX

I yet my silent judgment keep,
Disputing not what they believe:
But sure as oft as women weep,
It is to be suppos'd they grieve.

MUSIC'S EMPIRE

FIRST WAS the world as one great cymbal made,
Where jarring winds to infant Nature plaid;
All musick was a solitary sound,
To hollow rocks and murm'ring fountains bound.

Jubal first made the wilder notes agree,
And Jubal tuned Musick's jubilee;
He call'd the ecchoes from their sullen cell,
And built the organ's city, where they dwell.

Each sought a consort in that lovely place,
And virgin trebles wed the manly base,
From whence the progeny of numbers new
Into harmonious colonies withdrew;

Some to the lute, some to the viol went,
And others chose the cornet eloquent;
These practising the wind, and those the wire,
To sing man's triumphs, or in heaven's choir.

Then Musick, the mosaique of the air,
Did of all these a solemn noise prepare,
With which she gain' d the empire of the ear,
Including all between the earth and sphear.

Victorious sounds! yet here your homage do
Unto a gentler conqueror than you;
Who, though he flies the musick of his praise,
Would with you heaven's hallelujahs raise.

ANDREW MARVELL

from THE CHARACTER OF HOLLAND

HOLLAND, that scarce deserves the name of land,
  As but th' off-scouring of the British sand;
And so much earth as was contributed
By English pilots when they heav'd the lead;
Or what by th' ocean's slow alluvion fell,
Of shipwrack'd cockle and the mussel-shell;
This indigested vomit of the sea
Fell to the Dutch by just propriety.

Glad then, as miners that have found the ore,
They with mad labour fish'd the land to shore;
And div'd as desperately for each piece
Of earth, as if't had been of ambergris;
Collecting anxiously small loads of clay,
Less than what building swallows bear away;
Or than those pills which sordid beetles roll,
Transfusing into them their dunghill soul.

How did they rivet, with gigantic piles,
Thorough the centre their new-catched miles;
And to the stake a struggling country bound,
Where barking waves still bait the forced ground;
Building their watry Babel far more high
To reach the sea, than those to scale the sky.

Yet still his claim the injur'd ocean laid,
And oft at leap-frog ore their steeples play'd:
As if on purpose it on land had come
To show them what's their *mare liberum*.
A daily deluge over them does boil;

The earth and water play at level-coil;
The fish oft-times the burgher dispossest,
And sat not as a meat but as a guest;
And oft the Tritons and the sea-nymphs saw
Whole sholes of Dutch serv'd up for cabillau;
Or as they over the new level rang'd
For pickled *herring*, pickled *heeren* chang'd.
Nature, it seem'd, asham'd of her mistake,
Would throw their land away at duck and drake.

TO HIS NOBLE FRIEND, MR RICHARD LOVELACE, UPON HIS POEMS

Sir,

Ovr times are much degenerate from those
Which your sweet Muse, which your fair Fortune chose;
And as complexions alter with the Climes,
Our wits have drawne th'infection of our times,
That candid Age no other way could tell
To be ingenious, but by speaking well.
Who best could prayse, had then the greatest prayse;
'Twas more esteemd to give than wear the bayes.
Modest ambition studi'd only then
To honour not her selfe, but worthy men.
These vertues now are banisht out of Towne,
Our Civill Wars have lost the Civicke crowne.
He highest builds, who with most Art destroys,
And against others Fame his owne employs.
I see the envious Caterpillar sit
On the faire blossome of each growing wit.
   The Ayre's already tainted with the swarms
Of Insects, which against you rise in arms.
Word-peckers, Paper-Rats, Book-scorpions,

ANDREW MARVELL

Of wit corrupted, the unfashion'd Sons.
The barbèd Censurers begin to looke
Like the grim consistory on thy Booke;
And on each line cast a reforming eye
Severer than the yong Presbytery.
Till when in vaine they have thee all perus'd,
You shall for being faultlesse be accus'd.
Some reading your *Lucasta* will alledge
You wrong'd in her the Houses Priviiledge;
Some that you under sequestration are,
Because you write when going to the Warre;
And one the Book prohibits, because Kent
Their first Petition by the Authour sent.
   But when the beauteous Ladies came to know,
That their deare Lovelace was endanger'd so:
Lovelace, that thaw'd the most congealed brest,
He who lov'd best, and them defended best,
Whose hand so rudely grasps the steely brand,
Whose hand so gently melts the Ladies hand,
They all in mutiny, though yet undrest,
Sally'd, and would in his defence contest.
And one, the loveliest that was yet e're seen,
Thinking that I too of the rout had been,
Mine eyes invaded with a female spight
(She knew what pain't would be to lose that sight).
O no, mistake not, I reply'd: for I
In your defence, or in his cause would dy:
But he, secure of glory and of time,
Above their envy or mine aid doth clime.
Him valianst men and fairest Nymphs approve,
His Booke in them finds Judgement, with you, Love.

AN HORATIAN ODE UPON CROMWELL'S RETURN FROM IRELAND

THE FORWARD youth that would appeare,
Must now forsake his Muses deare,
    Nor in the shadows sing
    His numbers languishing.

'Tis time to leave the books in dust,
And oyle th'unused armour's rust;
    Removing from the wall
    The corselett of the hall.

So restlesse Cromwell could not cease
In the inglorious arts of peace,
    But through adventures warre
    Urged his active starre;

And, like the three-forked lightning, first
Breaking the clouds where it was nurst,
    Did through his own Side
    His fiery way divide:

(For 'tis all one to courage high,
The emulous, or enemy;
    And with such, to enclose,
    Is more than to oppose;)

Then burning through the aire he went,
And palaces and temples rent;
    And Caesar's head at last
    Did through his laurels blast.

'Tis madness to resist or blame
The face of angry heaven's flame;
    And if we would speak true,
    Much to the man is due,

ANDREW MARVELL

Who from his private gardens, where
He lived reserved and austere,
    As if his highest plott
    To plant the bergamott,

Could by industrious valour climb
To ruin the great work of Time,
    And cast the kingdoms old,
    Into another mould.

Though Justice against Fate complaine,
And plead the antient rights in vaine;
    But those do hold or breake,
    As men are strong or weake:

Nature, that hateth emptinesse,
Allows of penetration lesse,
    And therefore must make roome,
    Where greater spirits come.

What field of all the Civil Warre
Where his were not the deepest scarre?
    And Hampton shows what part
    He had of wiser art,

Where, twining subtile fears with hope,
He wove a net of such a scope
    That Charles himself might chase
    To Caresbrook's narrow case,

That thence the royal actor borne
The tragic scaffold might adorne;
    While round the armed bands
    Did clap their bludy hands

He nothing common did or mean,
Upon that memorable scene,
But with his keener eye
The axe's edge did trye;

Nor called the gods, with vulgar spight,
To vindicate his helplesse right;
But bowed his comely head
Downe, as upon a bed.

This was that memorable houre,
Which first assured the forced power:
So when they did designe
The capitol's first line,

A Bleeding Head, where they begun,
Did fright the architects to run;
And yet in that the State
Foresaw its happy fate!

And now the Irish are asham'd
To see themselves in one year tarn'd:
So much one man can doe
That does both act and know.

They can affirme his praises best,
And have, though overcome, confest
How good he is, how just,
And fit for highest trust

Nor yet grown stiffer with command,
But still in the Republick's hand—
How fit he is to sway,
That can so well obey!

He to the Commons' feet presents
A kingdom for his first year's rents,
    And (what he may) forbears
    His fame, to make it theirs:

And has his sword and spoyls ungirt
To lay them at the publick's skirt:
    So when the falcon high
    Falls heavy from the skigh,

She, having kill'd, no more doth search,
But on the next green bough to perch,
    Where, when he first does lure,
    The faulkner has her sure.

—What may not then our Isle presume,
While victory his crest does plume?
    What may not others feare,
    If thus he crowns each yeare?

As Caesar, he, ere long, to Gaul,
To Italy an Hannibal,
    And to all States not free,
    Shall clymaterick be.

The Pict no shelter now shall find
Within his party-colour' d mind,
    But, from this valour sad,
    Shrink underneath the plaid—

Happy, if in the tufted brake,
The English hunter him mistake,
    Nor lay his hounds in neere
    The Caledonian deer.

But thou, the Warr's and Fortune's sonne,
March indefatigably on;
 And for the last effect,
 Still keep the sword erect:

Besides the force it has to fright
The spirits of the shady night,
 The same arts that did gain
 A pow'r must it maintain.